FAITH
IN FRIENDSHIP

My Friend Is
Buddhist

by Tamra Orr

PURPLE TOAD
PUBLISHING

FAITH IN FRIENDSHIP

My Friend Is Buddhist
My Friend Is Christian
My Friend Is Hindu
My Friend Is Jewish
My Friend Is Muslim

Printing 1 2 3 4 5 6 7 8 9

Publisher's Cataloging-in-Publication Data
Orr, Tamra.
  My friend is buddhist / written by Tamra Orr.
    p. cm.
Includes bibliographic references and index.
ISBN 9781624691102
1. Buddhism—Juvenile literature. 2. Religious life—Buddhism. I. Series: Faith in friendship
BQ4032 2015
294.3
                                                    2014945182
eBook ISBN: 9781624691119

Contents

Chapter One: Hello! My Name Is Ashoka 5

    Metta Sutta 9

Chapter Two: The Birth of Buddha............................ 11

    Four Centuries Ago 17

Chapter Three: The Eightfold Path 19

    Buddhist Celebrations................................. 27

Chapter Four: Reincarnation, Meditation,

    and Mantras 29

    The Dalai Lama... 35

Chapter Five: Buddhists Today 37

    Celebrity Buddhists 41

Timeline... 42

Chapter Notes 42

Further Reading 44

    Books.. 44

    Works Consulted 44

    On the Internet... 45

Glossary 46

Index 47

Ashoka touring his new school.

Hello! My Name Is Ashoka

I walked into the gymnasium with my parents close behind me. There must have been over a hundred people inside, many of them lined up in front of tables full of food. This was the first "Back to School Night" I had ever attended. In China, there was nothing like it. I had moved to Oregon over the summer. I had counted the days until school started. Would it be exciting—or scary? Would I love going to an American school—or wish I could go back home? My family had moved here because my uncle lives in Portland and he had found a job for my father in his electronics business. We had always heard that life in America was wonderful, and so far, it seemed true. My family and I loved the Pacific Northwest. I could not stop looking at the mountains, and I recently visited the ocean for the first time. There was blue water as far as the eye could see. I think I could have watched the waves for hours.

Now it was time to go to school and see what American classrooms were like. This huge room we were in was called a gym, I was told. The floor was made of shiny wood. At each end was a basketball hoop that seemed impossibly tall. Brown wooden benches were folded up against the walls.

The room was buzzing with the sound of countless voices. I had learned English in school as a young child. I thought I spoke it well. However, it was one thing to use it in the classroom with other students, and another to be surrounded by a roar of words tossed back and forth so effortlessly. I began to doubt myself. If I felt this awkward, I knew my parents were probably quite uncomfortable.

"Mr. and Mrs. Seng, hello!" said a loud voice behind us. We turned to see Principal Chamberlain standing there, his hand outstretched. "Welcome to Lincoln Elementary School. We are so glad to place Ashoka in Mrs. Hooper's fourth-grade class." My parents shook hands with the principal. "Please, help yourselves to the food before the program begins," he said, pointing at the rows of casseroles, snacks, desserts, and salads. I had never seen so much food in one place before. I was torn between nervousness and hunger. It only took a few seconds before hunger won!

My mother, father, and I lined up with the others. As I reached for a plate, a boy about my age walked up and stood next to me. "Hey," he said, "I'm Daniel. You're new, right?" I nodded. "You should have some of that ham casserole right there," he added, pointing. "My mom made it and it's great."

I took a deep breath, and then said, "Hello, Mr. Daniel. My name is Ashoka. My family does not eat meat, but I am sure your mother's cass . . . casserole is quite tasty."

"Oh, man, you don't eat meat?" said Daniel. I froze. Had I already done something wrong? Was Daniel about to walk away muttering about the weird new boy who wouldn't eat a bite of ham? "So, why not?" he asked.

My mother (third from left) enjoys chatting with the teachers and other mothers at Back to School Night.

"Is it your health? Your morals? Concern for the environment?" He looked closely at me and then shook his head. "Nope! You don't look like a hippie."

I laughed. "No, I'm not a hippie, Mr. Daniel. I'm a Buddhist. We do not eat meat."

Daniel paused, and then said, "Oh—okay. In that case, come over here to this table. It has nothing but vegetarian food. Oh, and please drop the 'mister.' We only use that for grownups." He smiled.

My parents and I were shocked to see platter after platter of dishes that did not have any meat in them. "Welcome to Portland, Oregon," said Daniel. "At least half of our class is vegetarian for one reason or another. But so far, I think you're our first Buddhist!"

After we got our food, Daniel and I sat down together, while all of the parents went to the auditorium to listen to Principal Chamberlain speak. "So, you're a Buddhist," said Daniel. "I've never met one before. You worship a god named Buddha, right?"

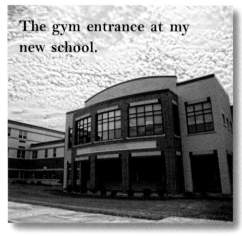

The gym entrance at my new school.

"No," I said, shaking my head. "Many people think that is true, but Buddhists do not worship anyone. Buddha was not a god. He was just a man—a very wise man."

"So what do you do when you go to church?" asked Daniel.

I smiled. "We don't go to church exactly. We have shrines at home where we go to pray instead. If we do go to a temple, we do it mainly to give food to the monks that live there. We also take flowers, candles, and incense to the statues of Buddha."

"Do you go to your temple on any special day of the week, like Saturday or Sunday?"

"No. We go whenever we want to," I replied. I knew that probably sounded very odd to Daniel. To my surprise, he was not looking at me like I was strange at all. Instead, he was looking at me like I was really interesting.

"I'm confused," admitted Daniel. "If you don't have a god, why do you pray?"

"We pray to remind ourselves to follow Buddha's rules and the ways of the Noble Eightfold Path," I explained. Daniel only looked more confused.

"The Eight . . . what?"

"The Noble Eightfold Path," I answered. I sighed. There was no way to explain centuries of Buddhism over a plate of chocolate chip cookies and a cup of apple juice. "Daniel, I would be happy to tell you all about my faith, but let's do it slowly, so it makes more sense. Perhaps I could have lunch with you tomorrow in the cafeteria, and I can start at the beginning. That is . . ." I hesitated, ". . . if you really are interested in knowing more."

"Great!" said Daniel, jumping to his feet. "My parents are calling me, so I have to go anyway. I'll see you tomorrow at lunch, Ashoka."

I waved goodbye and looked down at my almost empty plate. First, vegetarian food, then a new friend—and even a chance to talk about Buddhism. What a great first day!

The Metta Sutta

Buddha taught many lessons on how to live life to its fullest. One of his most famous is the Metta Sutta. The word *metta* is sometimes translated as "loving kindness;" and the Metta Sutta is a guide for people to learn to love others. It explains the conditions a person must meet in order to allow the loving kindness to grow in their mind and heart.

This is what should be done by one who is skilled in goodness
And who knows the path of peace:
Let them be able and upright, straightforward and gentle in speech,
Humble and not conceited, contented and easily satisfied.
Unburdened with duties and frugal in their ways.
Peaceful and calm, and wise and skilful,
not proud and demanding in nature.
Let them not do the slightest thing that the wise would later reprove.
They should wish:

 In gladness and in safety
 May all beings be at ease.
 Whatever living beings there may be,
 Whether they are weak or strong, omitting none,
 The great or the mighty, medium, short or small,
 The seen and the unseen,
 Those living near and far away,
 Those born and to-be-born,
 May all beings be at ease!

Let none deceive another, or despise any being in any state,
Let none through anger or ill-will wish harm upon another.
Even as a mother protects with her life her child, her only child,
So with a boundless heart should one cherish all living beings,
Radiating kindness over the entire world,
Spreading upwards to the skies, and downwards to the depths,
Outwards and unbounded, freed from hatred and ill-will.
Whether standing or walking, seated or lying down,
Free from drowsiness, one should sustain this recollection.[1]

The first day of school is loud and busy!

The Birth of Buddha

My first day at school was crazy, loud, and great fun. I loved the noise of the hallways, including the slam of locker doors, the river of voices, the occasional bell, and the chirp of everyone's cell phones. By the time the lunch hour came, I was hungry and ready to see a familiar face. I looked across the cafeteria and saw Daniel waving at me, motioning me over to his table.

"Hey, Ashoka! How was your first morning at school?" he asked as I sat down.

"Surprisingly smooth," I replied. "Look, I even found enough to eat in your cafeteria. They have an amazing salad bar. I am grateful so many Portlanders do not eat meat, even if it means they are hippies."

Daniel laughed. "I'm glad, too. Now where were we yesterday?"

"Before I tell you all about Buddhism, I think you should know how it began, Mr. . . . I mean, Daniel. Sit back, and let me tell you a story."

I took a picture of Daniel on my phone. He taught me the peace sign.

Putting his feet up on a chair, Daniel stretched out, prepared to listen.

"Once upon a time, in 563 BCE, a prince was born in Nepal near the base of the Himalaya Mountains," I began. "His name was Siddhartha Gautama.[1] As a child, it was predicted that he would grow up to either be a rich king, or a very wise leader. Since the king wanted his son to grow up and take his place, he did not allow the young prince out of the palace. Siddhartha grew up, got married at 16 to his cousin, and had a son. He was rich and powerful. When he was 29 years old, the prince left the palace for the very first time. He saw astounding things. First, he saw a man who was very, very old and covered in wrinkles. He had never seen old age before. Next, he saw a very sick woman. He had never seen illness. Finally, he saw a funeral procession. He had never seen death."

"That was one sheltered prince," Daniel chimed in.

"Siddhartha was overwhelmed. He had never seen such unhappiness. Then, he met a holy man. The man had nothing, yet he was happy. It was confusing to the prince. Finally, he decided to leave his palace, his riches, and even his family to go and search for the answers to life's questions.

"For years, Siddhartha wandered, talking to people, looking for answers. He lived with monks in a monastery. He was on the streets, begging for food for over six years. One day, he finally sat down under a bodhi tree. Siddhartha closed his eyes and meditated for a long time."

"Meditated? What does that mean?" asked Daniel.

"It means sitting still and calming your mind for a very long time," I explained. "You focus your thinking as you relax your body. Siddhartha meditated for forty-nine days and nights."

"Wait a minute! forty-nine days? Didn't he have to stop to eat and drink?"

The Legend states that Siddhartha reached enlightenment after seven weeks.

"The legend says he fasted. Finally, he realized the answer to finding happiness."

"Really?" Daniel sat up straight and leaned toward me. "What was it?"

"He said he had discovered Four Noble Truths," I explained. "The first is that life means suffering. The second is that the reason people suffer is because they have been greedy and selfish. They always want more and more and are never satisfied with what they have.[2]

"The third truth is that suffering is not necessary," I continued. "And the fourth truth is that happiness is also possible through acceptance and appreciation of what you already have, and from helping others. The prince called these Four Noble Truths 'enlightenment.' He expressed it as 'Abandon negative action; Create perfect virtue; Subdue your own mind. This is the teaching of the Buddha.'[3]

"And, after that, Siddhartha changed his name to Buddha, which means 'the enlightened one,'" I concluded. [4]

"That is a really good story," said Daniel. "Thanks for telling me about it. So, Buddha was . . . a man? A really wise man, but without any superpowers or anything?"

"I am glad you asked that question," I said, grinning at the idea of the Buddha wearing a cape and mask. "There is a famous story about Buddha being asked that exact same thing. People asked him, 'Are you a god?' And he said, 'No.' So they asked, 'Are you an angel?' 'No,' he said again. 'A saint perhaps?' asked another. 'No,' he said one more time. 'Then what are you?' they demanded. The Buddha patiently replied, 'I am awake.'"[5]

"What a cool answer," said Daniel. "I am awake. . . . I like that."

"After Buddha was enlightened," I continued, "he went back to the monks he had lived with before and taught the lessons he had learned while he meditated. They, in turn, taught others. Slowly, the message spread from country to country. Hundreds of monks told the tale of the Buddha and what he had discovered. Soon, there were followers of Buddha throughout India, Cambodia, Japan, Korea, Vietnam, Laos, Sri Lanka, Thailand, and my home country, China.

"Today, Buddhists make five promises or precepts," I added.

Not eating animals is a large part of Buddhism.

"Who are they promising?" asked Daniel.

"Buddha and themselves, I guess," I replied.

"What are the promises?"

I pulled out a notebook from my backpack and opened it up to the first page. I always wrote the precepts down and carried them with me as reminders.

"The first one is to abstain from taking the lives of living beings," I said.

"Abstain?" asked Daniel.

"It means to give up or not do," I replied.

"So abstaining from taking the lives of living beings is why you are a vegetarian?"

I nodded.

"What about bugs? You know, mosquitoes, spiders, ants, and so on?"

"Even those we try not to kill," I said.

"Wow!" Daniel exclaimed. "That is amazing! I am not sure I could do that. So, what is the second promise?"

I pointed to my notebook. "To abstain from taking that which is not yours."

"In other words, don't steal?" he asked.

Buddhists believe in preserving life, even those of insects.

"Yes, but it means more than that," I said. "It also means not withholding the truth from someone, or returning something you once borrowed. It can even mean not cheating when you are playing a game."

"That sounds like one of the Christian Commandments, 'Thou shalt not steal.' What is the third promise?"

"Not to be greedy, or want more than you already have."

"I remember that idea from your story earlier," Daniel said.

"The fourth promise is that you will not lie, which includes gossiping or not thinking about how your words may affect another person. And the last promise is that you will not use anything that threatens or poisons your ability to think clearly, such as alcohol or drugs. Buddhists do not smoke cigarettes or drink coffee for the same reason," I added.

"That's incredible!" said Daniel. "Those are a lot of big, important promises. Do you have any trouble sticking to them?"

I shook my head. Daniel certainly asked some interesting questions. "Most of the time I don't," I said. "But now and then I catch myself wanting something—like a new cell phone."

"So, what do you do when that happens?"

"I do what all Buddhists are supposed to do. I pray for wisdom, meditate, and follow the guidance of Buddha."

Just then, I spotted an ant crawling across the lunch table. Daniel saw it too and raised his hand to kill it. I caught his eye. He stopped and then let the ant go on its way. I smiled. "You're a great student, Daniel," I said.

Suddenly, the lunch bell rang and I knew that meant I had three minutes to get to my next class. I grabbed my notebook and stuffed it into my backpack.

"Hey!" said Daniel. "We still didn't get to that Noble Path thing."

"Let's meet for lunch again tomorrow," I said, rushing down the hallway. "Remember, I don't lie!"

Four Centuries Ago

In Northern India, King Ashoka (reigned 269–232 BCE), for whom Ashoka was named, was the first to write about Buddhism. He wrote messages about this wonderful new philosophy on rocks and pillars, and showed how he began following the morals of Buddhism in order to rule with justice and compassion. In history, King Ashoka was considered such an impressive leader that historian H. G. Wells wrote, "Amidst the tens of thousands of names of monarchs that crowd the columns of history . . . the name of Ashoka shines, and shines almost alone, a star."[6]

During the mid-1800s, Buddhism reached Europe and poets like Ralph Waldo Emerson and Walt Whitman, as well as essayist Henry David Thoreau, were fascinated by it. They used Buddhist concepts to write some of their most well-known poems and essays. In 1893, some Buddhist monks spoke at the Chicago World's Fair. So many people there were impressed by the message that the philosophy began to spread.[7]

Ashoka

17

Meditation is much easier to do in a quiet, peaceful location.

The Eightfold Path

My second day of class was not quite as smooth as the first. I had gotten lost twice and completely forgot my locker combination. I was more than ready to sit down in the cafeteria with Daniel and relax for a little while. What I really wanted to do was find a quiet place and meditate for a few minutes. I knew it would calm me down and I would have the chance to connect with the Buddha's lessons about focus and patience. I could not imagine a place anywhere around the school that would allow me that much privacy.

Just as I started eating my salad, Daniel slid into the chair across from me.

"Ready when you are, Ashoka!" he said with a grin.

"Ready for what?"

"For your Noble Path lesson," he chuckled. "Do you have them written down?"

I blushed and nodded. "Yes, I carry them with me as reminders, too. These eight 'rights,' as they are called, are how each person can become enlightened like the Buddha. They bring an end to suffering."

"Let's hear it," said Daniel.

"The first one is referred to as 'right view,' " I said. "Basically, the Buddha is saying you have to know that suffering happens, but it does not have to happen if you choose otherwise. You have to have the right attitude."

"I hear about attitude all the time at home," replied Daniel.

"The second is called 'right intention' and that means it has to be important to you to make the effort to 'wake up' and help other people," I explained. "It requires that you make a real commitment to improving yourself. The third and fourth steps are 'right speech' and 'right action.' If you remember the promises you make not to lie or say unkind things, this is similar. You must remember to speak and act kindly and avoid hurting

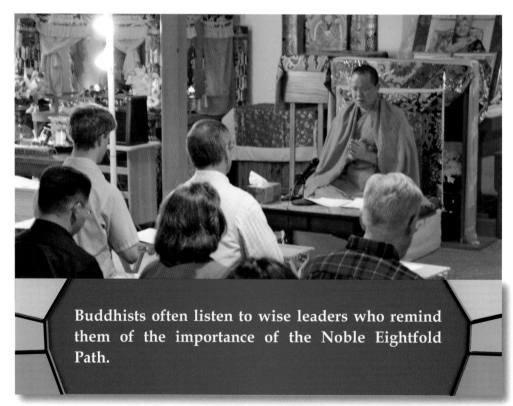

Buddhists often listen to wise leaders who remind them of the importance of the Noble Eightfold Path.

If someone yells at you, you must try not to yell back

anyone with your words or actions. The Buddha truly believed that words break or save lives, make enemies or friends, start war or create peace."[1]

"That is a great lesson that I wish some of the people at this school would learn," agreed Daniel.

"The next right is 'right livelihood' and it means that each person finds work that is useful, meaningful, and expresses who they are and what they care about in this world," I described.

"That can be really hard, I think," said Daniel. "I know many adults who have no idea what they want to do with their lives."

"You're right, Daniel, that is one of the hardest steps. However, the Buddha tells us that if we meditate about it and think about it, the direction to go in will become much clearer. He said we should never have jobs that deal with weapons, or hurt living things, either as farmers or in slaughterhouses. Buddhists are not to work for anyone who sells alcohol or drugs either.

"Once that livelihood is chosen, the next step is 'right effort,' or putting all of our energy and beliefs into our jobs and what we do with our lives. The last two parts of the eightfold path are 'right mindfulness' and 'right concentration.' Being mindful just means paying close attention to how we live our lives," I said.

"You mean—look at what is happening in our lives and see if changes need to be made?" asked Daniel.

"Exactly! You are a fantastic learner, Daniel," I exclaimed.

"Oh, yeah? Would you please tell my teachers that, Ashoka?" he asked with a grin. "They might have a slightly different opinion. So what does 'right concentration' mean?"

"This is the ability to remain calm and focus on what we need to do to help ourselves stay on the path, and help others who may need us. And those," I said with a flourish, "are the parts of the Noble Eightfold Path. Do you feel at least a little bit enlightened?"[2]

"Maybe. . . . So do you have to do each of these steps in exactly that order?" asked Daniel.

"Not at all," I replied. "They are more like individual strands in a thread that wind together in no particular order. Each one supports another."

"It feels like facts are leaking out of my ears now," said Daniel. "Thanks for all of the information. I'll be thinking about it for days."

He reached out and turned the pages of my notebook, and saw my drawings. "What are these?" he asked.

"These are some of the symbols of Buddhism," I explained. "This one is a lotus flower. It comes in many colors, and it represents purity. Legend says that when the Buddha was a baby, as he took his first steps, a lotus flower arose out of the ground with every step he took."

"What about this one?" Daniel asked. "It looks like a ship's wheel."

"It is. Its name is *dharmachakra* and it is a representation of the Noble Eightfold Path."[3]

Lotus blossom

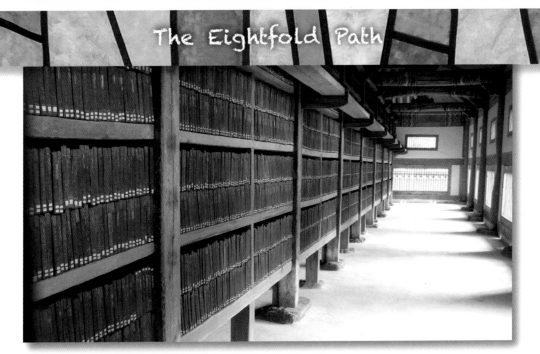

The Haeinsa Temple in South Korea holds 81,340 carved woodblocks of the complete Buddhist scriptures.

Daniel sat back and sighed. Immediately, I was worried. Had I bored him? Was he tired of me? Seeing the look on my face, he smiled. "No worries, Ashoka. I'm just trying to take it all in . . . four noble truths, five promises, an eightfold path . . . I feel like I'm in math class again."

We both laughed, and then Daniel paused. "Do you use a book like the Bible or the Koran to learn from?"

"We do," I replied. "One is called the Tripitaka, which means 'three baskets.' It is a collection of many writings about the Buddha and fills almost 50 volumes."

"Wow! That's a lot of reading. Why is it called the 'three baskets'?"

I smiled. "When the words were first written, there was no paper. Instead, the messages were written on long, narrow leaves. They were sewn together in bunches. These were stored inside—"[4]

"Baskets, right?" interrupted Daniel. I nodded.

"The Buddhist writing I like most are the Jataka Tales. There are over 500 of these stories and fables. My mother tells me one each night, for they teach important lessons."

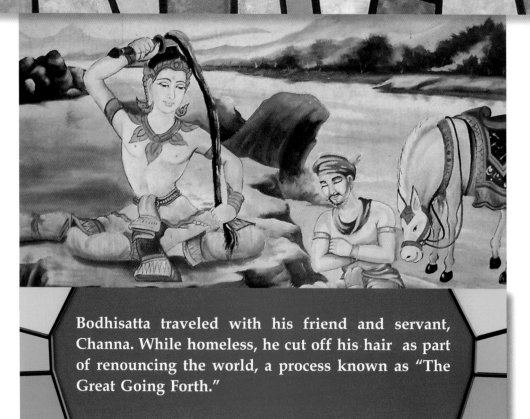

Bodhisatta traveled with his friend and servant, Channa. While homeless, he cut off his hair as part of renouncing the world, a process known as "The Great Going Forth."

"Can you give me an example of one?" Daniel asked. I suspected he would ask, so I was ready to tell him one of my favorites, *The Golden Mallard.*

"This is the tale of the Golden Mallard—a duck," I added when I saw the look on his face. "Once upon a time Bodhisatta—he is the main person in all the tales and is a special being—grew up and got married. He had three daughters named Nanda, Nanda-vati, and Sundari-nanda. When it was his time to die, Bodhisatta was surrounded by family and friends. He died, and was born again into the world as a golden mallard who remembered all the lives he had before." I stopped when I saw Daniel's frown.

"He died and came back to life?" he asked. I sighed. I had forgotten to discuss this part of Buddhism with him. "We will cover that idea later," I said, "but for now, just listen to the story."

The story of the Golden Mallard was always a favorite one of mine.

"As the duck grew, his feathers came in golden! One day he flew over his old house and saw that his wife and daughters were struggling to survive. He thought, 'I could give them a golden feather to use for money. I have so many feathers, I could take care of them for a long time.' He flew down to the house and right away, his wife and daughters asked who he was and where he had come from. The duck told them he was their father and he was there to help them."

"A talking duck?" asked Daniel.

"Don't your fairy tales and fables have talking animals in them?" I replied. Daniel sheepishly nodded.

"Anyway, he gave the women a feather. From time to time, he would return with another one. The women sold these feathers and grew wealthy.

"One day, the mother said to her daughters, 'We do not know how long your father will keep coming back. Perhaps he will fly away and forget us. Next time he brings us a feather, let's pick him clean!'"

At first, Bodhisatta looked like a natural mallard. He grew golden feathers, then turned pure white.

"Uh-oh," muttered Daniel.

"The next time the mallard came back, the wife grabbed him and took every one of his feathers. He could not fly. He was tossed into a barrel. As time went by, his feathers grew back, but they were plain white feathers of no value. One day he flew away and never came back again."[5]

"This story is a reminder not to be greedy, right?" asked Daniel.

"Yes!"

Just then the lunch bell rang. "Daniel, would you like to come to my house this weekend?" I asked shyly. "You could see the shrine we have in our home and we could talk more."

"Yeah, that sounds great!" he replied. "I also want you to teach me how to meditate."

Oh, goodness, I thought. This is going to be interesting.

Buddhist Celebrations

Each year, during the full moon in May, Buddhists across the world celebrate Vesak Day (or Wesak). The day marks Buddha's birthday, his moment of enlightenment, and his death. In South Korea and Sri Lanka, people release lanterns made of paper and wood into the sky. In Singapore, caged birds are released to symbolize freedom. In China, dancing dragons parade down city streets. Buddhists go to their temples to hear lessons, and to bring flowers, food, and candles to the monks living there.[6]

During Vesak Day, Buddhists sing and chant. They also pour water over the shoulders of Buddha statues. The water is a reminder to keep one's mind free of greed, hatred, and ignorance. Gifts are given to the Buddha to show respect and gratitude.[7]

Another important celebration for Buddhists is Nirvana Day. It is usually celebrated on February 15th (sometimes February 8th). The day is a reminder of the moment when the Buddha reached Nirvana, or the end of the cycle of birth and rebirth, at the age of 80. Many Buddhists dedicate the day to meditation or spending the day in Buddhist monasteries. The focus of Nirvana Day reflects how a person is spending his or her life; and accepting the fact that loss and change are natural elements of life, not reasons for sadness.[8]

Vesak is marked by May's full moon.

Some shrines are quite elaborate, and feature seats for meditators.

Reincarnation, Meditation, and Mantras

I woke Saturday morning to gray skies and rain tapping my window. I didn't mind though. Daniel was visiting today. We were going to play a new game on my computer, plus he was going to play some of his favorite music for me to see if I liked it. At some point, we would look at my family's shrine. I still needed to explain the concept of reincarnation, or rebirth—and teach Daniel how to meditate. It was going to be a long, busy day.

Before he came over, I showered, had breakfast and then spent time in my room meditating. I wanted to honor Buddha by accurately sharing his ideas with my new friend. I wanted to say the right things and be patient. When I was finished, I felt refreshed and ready for a great day with Daniel.

For the first three hours, we barely moved from in front of the computer. We played my game, and then I had a great time listening to some of his favorite music groups. After having a snack in the kitchen and formally meeting my parents, Daniel asked me about the duck in the story I had told the other day.

"How could a man die and come back to life as a duck?" he asked.

"Buddhists believe in reincarnation," I replied. Before he could ask, I added, "I will explain, but first, have you ever heard of karma?"

"Of course . . . it's the idea of what goes around comes around, right? Kids are saying that all the time."

"That is the popular concept of karma," I said. "To Buddhists, karma is the idea that if you do good things with your life—if you are generous and kind and you follow the ideas of Buddha—you will receive good karma. If

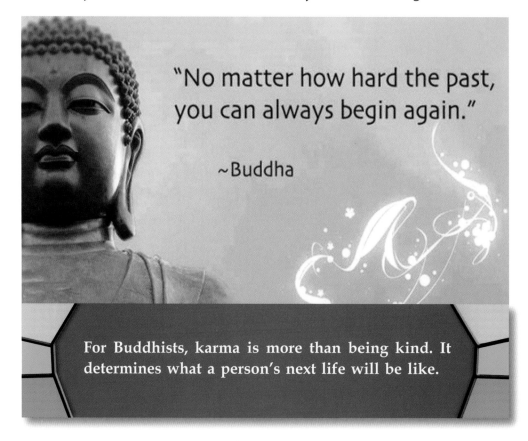

"No matter how hard the past, you can always begin again."

~Buddha

For Buddhists, karma is more than being kind. It determines what a person's next life will be like.

you lie, hurt others, or bring about unhappiness, you will receive bad karma."[1]

"I understand that," replied Daniel.

"As Buddhists, we believe that when we die, our positive or negative karma determines how we will return to Earth. If we led good lives, we will probably return as humans, or animals with special abilities."

"Like a duck with golden feathers?"

I nodded. "Those with bad karma, however, often come back as lower animals like snails or as ghosts who cannot find peace. The Buddha said," I recalled from memory,

Life is a journey
Death is a return to Earth
The universe is like an inn.
The passing years are like dust.
Regard this phantom world
As a star at dawn, a bubble in a stream,
A flash of lightning in a summer cloud
A flickering lamp—a phantom—and a dream.[2]

"The best way I can describe the Buddha's idea of rebirth is it is like lighting one candle by using the flame of the candle lit before it," I continued. "They are connected but each flame and each candle is unique. This process happens hundreds, even thousands of times. One is born, dies, and is reborn until he finally reaches enlightenment. Then the cycle ends. Does that make sense?"

Daniel nodded slowly. "I think so. Wow, that sure would make you want to do good things, huh? I mean, who wants to be a snail?"

I laughed. I loved how Daniel looked at things.

Next, I showed him our family's shrine. It was in a corner of our living room and had a curtain in front of it to set it aside. "We come here at least once a day," I explained. Inside was a very high shelf, decorated in gold. On it sat our Buddha statue we had brought over with us from China.

"Why is the shelf so high?" Daniel asked.

"That is to show honor. Nothing is ever placed above it to show that we respect the Buddha as our highest teacher."[3]

Inside the shrine, my family also had candlesticks, an incense burner, and vases with fresh flowers in them. These are often referred to as the "Three Treasures." I explained to Daniel that candles symbolize driving out the darkness from one's heart. Incense is lit to remind us that light is only found through good acts. Flowers are there to remind us that life is temporary, like the life span of a flower.

"What do you do when you come to the shrine?" asked Daniel in a whisper.

"First, we kneel down and light a candle and incense," I said. "Then we put our hands together with palms touching at the level of our hearts or higher. Often we chant and we always remember to move slowly, and gracefully. We lower our foreheads to the floor and place our palms about four to six inches apart. Then, we pray."

"For forgiveness?" asked Daniel.

"Not at all. Remember, the Buddha was not a god, but a teacher. We pray not to ask for something but to be reminded of his lessons and how we can become better Buddhists through his teachings."

I reached into the shrine and picked up a string of bright blue lapis beads. "This is my *mala*," I said. "I use it when I pray and meditate to help me focus and slow down my breathing."

"It's beautiful," said Daniel. "My Grandma Sylvia is Catholic and she has something like that that she calls a *rosary*."

"They are much the same," I agreed. "The Buddha would say that all religions are as one, so we often share ways of thinking and behaving."

"Is the shrine where you do your meditation?"

"No, we do that in our rooms usually," I replied. "Let's go back to my room and I will tell you about it."

Meditation is very meaningful to Buddhists and in my family, it often takes priority over everything, including meals and even homework! I knew there was no way I could fully explain to Daniel in just one afternoon why meditation was so important to my faith. I would just tell him the basics and let him explore more on his own if he wanted.

"Do you mediate sitting cross-legged on the floor with your hands making an O-shape?" asked Daniel.

"Sometimes," I replied. "But in Buddhism, meditation is not about how or where you sit. It is about what is going on in your mind. Meditation is good for the mind and the body. The Buddha believed that daily meditation makes it easier for us to be mindful people, and to be more at peace. I do it every morning before school, and every night before bed. It helps ensure that I have the right attitude."[4]

"I remember that—it is one of the rules on the Noble Eightfold Path, right?"

I high-fived Daniel for remembering that.

"Tell me how to meditate, Ashoka," he said.

"I like to sit cross-legged on the floor by my bed," I explained. "I get comfortable, and then I begin to say my personal mantra. A mantra is a word or phrase that is repeated over and over to help us relax and clear our minds. Some people count their breaths. Some say things like, 'Calmly let your breath fall away in exhalation and say to yourself 'one', then breathe in that 'one'. Breathe out again, and begin 'two'.[5] My mantra is just a phrase that focuses on peace."

Items on the shelf of our shrine to Buddha

When saying your mantra, pick any peaceful spot you choose, whether it is inside or out.

"What does it sound like?"

"Om śanti śanti śanti," I replied.[6]

Daniel repeated it to himself. "I like how it sounds," he said.

"Ashoka, Daniel's mother is here," my mother called from the kitchen. How fast the afternoon had gone! I had enjoyed every bit of it.

"Thanks for teaching me all about Buddhism, Ashoka," said Daniel. "I feel a lot smarter, plus I just like the idea of kindness and compassion. I've been thinking about it a lot. I even stopped myself from being grouchy at breakfast because I remembered you saying it is important not to say or do anything hurtful."

I am not sure I had ever felt as happy as I did at that moment. I felt like I had been a good Buddhist because I had shared the Buddha's beliefs and ideas with a friend—and that had to be good karma for us both.

The Dalai Lama

One of the greatest Buddhist leaders is the Dalai Lama, a name which means "teacher whose wisdom is as great as the ocean."[7] The very first was Gendun Drub, a man born in the late 14th century. Since then, there have been 13 others, with an average of two per century.

The 14th Dalai Lama was born in 1935 in northeastern Tibet. His name was Lhamo Thondup and was believed to be the reincarnation of the previous Dalai Lama, Thupten Gyatso. At the age of four, Thondup was named His Holiness Tenzin Gyatso. Like many young Buddhist boys in this part of the world, Gyatso joined a monastery when he was quite young.

The Dalai Lama has spent his life working for peace. He has been a spokesman for Buddhism and has written several books about it, including *The Art of Happiness, An Open Heart, Transforming the Mind*, and *How to Expand Love: Widening the Circle of Loving Relationships.* In 1989, he was awarded the Nobel Peace Prize. In recent years, the Dalai Lama joined MIT (Massachusetts Institute of Technology) to study the role of meditation in human emotion and knowledge. He said, "If science proves facts that conflict with Buddhist understanding, Buddhism must change accordingly. We should always adopt a view that accords with the facts."[8] As the Dalai Lama approached 78 years old, he traveled less and gave fewer speeches. He still focused on the beauty of peace. When he was in Portland, Oregon, in 2001, he spoke to 25,000 people in the city's Pioneer Courthouse Square. "Peace is not just mere absence of violence," he reminded the large crowd. "Peace is, I think, manifestation of human compassion."[9]

The Dalai Lama

Sharing my beliefs and my history was an exciting new part of being in a new school.

Buddhists Today

The weekend flew by, and it was already Monday morning again. I greeted the day with prayer and meditation, and then grabbed my homework and ran for the bus. The morning seemed to last about ten minutes, and then it was lunch time again. As I slid into my seat at my usual table, I was surprised to see Daniel there along with two other boys and a girl.

"This is Jonathan, Louis, and Pamela. I've been telling them about Buddhism," he quickly explained. "They are curious about it and I told them you'd answer their questions." He paused and then a worried look came over his face. "Is that all right, Ashoka?" he asked quietly.

I gave him a big smile and nod. While I felt a little overwhelmed by three new people at once, I was also happy to make more friends.

Jonathan, Louis, and Pamela showed me that answering and asking questions was one of the best parts of a school day.

"You're the first Buddhist I have ever met," said Pamela. "Don't you get lonely without other Buddhists around?"

"Actually, no," I said. "Portland has quite a few temples around and my parents have already been in contact with several of them. There are over two million Buddhists in the United States, and I have been told it is one of the fastest growing faiths in the country.[1] Also, my father is talking to the people at Maitripa College in Portland."

"What is Maitripa?" asked Louis.

"It is a graduate school on the east side of Portland that focuses on Buddhist studies," I replied. "The founder of the school combines study with meditation and community service. My father says that classes often end in chanting. I hope I can go there someday."[2]

"Chanting in class?" asked Jonathan. "Now that sounds like fun."

"Now, I have some questions for you guys," I said, after taking a deep, calming breath. "I've done nothing but talk about me, and the Buddha, since I got here. It's my turn."

Chanting is one of
the many skills
Buddhist monks
develop over time.

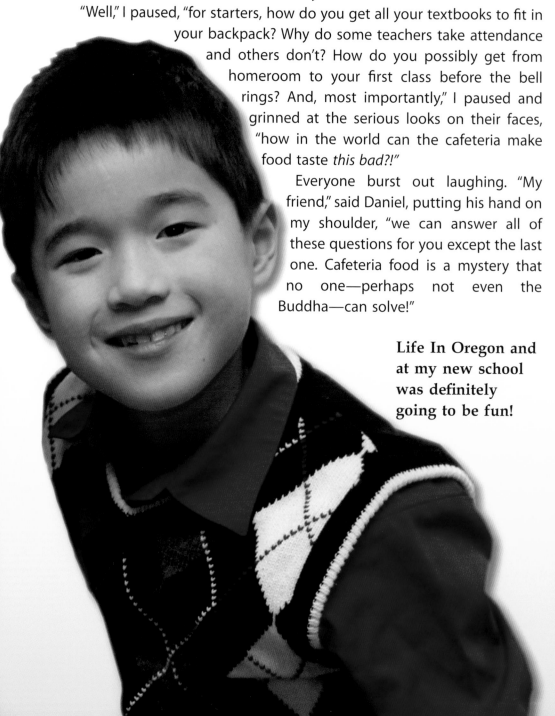

Louis, Pamela, Jonathan, and Daniel just looked at each other and then back at me. "Ask us what?" Daniel finally said.

"Well," I paused, "for starters, how do you get all your textbooks to fit in your backpack? Why do some teachers take attendance and others don't? How do you possibly get from homeroom to your first class before the bell rings? And, most importantly," I paused and grinned at the serious looks on their faces, "how in the world can the cafeteria make food taste *this bad?!*"

Everyone burst out laughing. "My friend," said Daniel, putting his hand on my shoulder, "we can answer all of these questions for you except the last one. Cafeteria food is a mystery that no one—perhaps not even the Buddha—can solve!"

Life In Oregon and at my new school was definitely going to be fun!

Celebrity Buddhists

As Buddhism has spread throughout the United States, a growing number of people, including celebrities, have practiced its techniques. Some of them are:

Brad Pitt (Actor)
Orlando Bloom (Actor)
Tina Turner (Singer)
Leonard Cohen (Singer-Songwriter)
Herbie Hancock (Jazz Musician)
Richard Gere (Actor)
Kate Bosworth (Actress)
George Lucas (Director)
Aung San Suu Kyi (Activist)[3]

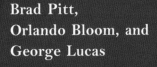

Brad Pitt,
Orlando Bloom, and
George Lucas

Chapter 5 Buddhists Today

1. Bill Aiken and Clark Strand. "A Reporter's Guide to Buddhism in America" (Santa Monica, CA: Soak Gakka International, 2005), http://www.sgi-usa.org/newsandevents/newsroom/americanbuddhist.pdf

2. Nancy Haught, p. L1.

3. Top 10 Celebrity Buddhists, http://www.wildmind.org/blogs/on-practice/top-10-celebrity-buddhists

Further Reading

Books

Cooper, Alison. *Facts about Buddhism*. New York: Rosen Central Publishing, 2010.

Gerner, Kathy. *Buddhism*. Tarrytown, NY: Marshall Cavendish Children's Books, 2008.

Gyatso, Geshe Kelsang. *What Is Buddhism?* Glen Spey, NY: Tharpa Publications, 2013.

Hawker, Frances, and Sunantha Phusomsai. *Buddhism in Thailand*. New York: Crabtree Publishing Company, 2009.

Landaw, Jonathan. *Prince Siddhartha: The Story of Buddha*. Somerville, MA: Wisdom Publications, 2011.

Nardo, Don. *Buddhism*. North Mankato, MN: Compass Point Books, 2009.

Thompson, Mel. *Buddhism*. Toronto, Canada: Whitecap Books, Ltd., 2010.

Whitney, Stewart. *Becoming Buddha: The Story of Siddhartha*. Torrance, CA: Heian Publishing, 2009.

Works Consulted

Aiken, Bill, and Clark Strand. "A Reporter's Guide to Buddhism in America." Santa Monica, CA: Soak Gakka International, 2005. http://www.sgi-usa.org/newsandevents/newsroom/americanbuddhist.pdf

Bodhi, Bhikkhu. "The Noble Eightfold Path: The Way to the End of Suffering." *AccesstoInsight.org*, 1999–2013. http://www.accesstoinsight.org/lib/authors/bodhi/waytoend.html#ch2

Chodron, Thubten. *Buddhism for Beginners*. Berkeley, CA: North Atlantic Books, 2001.

Cowell, E. B. editor. *The Jataka; or Stories of the Buddha's Former Births*. Cambridge: Cambridge University Press, 1901. http://www.pitt.edu/~dash/jataka.html#about

Dhammika, Ven S. "The Edicts of King Ashoka." Buddhist Publication Society, 1993. http://www.cs.colostate.edu/~malaiya/ashoka.html

Gach, Gary. *The Complete Idiot's Guide to Understanding Buddhism.* New York: Penguin Group, 2004.

Haught, Nancy. "Higher Learning in Buddhism." *The Sunday Oregonian,* 2013.

Huff Post Religion. "Vesak: How Buddha's Birthday Is Celebrated Around the World." *HuffingtonPost.com,* 2012. http://www.huffingtonpost.com/2012/05/05/vesak-how-buddhas-birthda_n_1478896.html

Khantipalo, Bhikkhu. "Lay Buddhist Practice: The Shrine Room, Uposatha Days, Rains Residence." *AccesstoInsight.org,* 1995. http://www.accesstoinsight.org/lib/authors/khantipalo/wheel206.html#shrine

Smith, Huston, and Philip Novak. *Buddhism: A Concise Introduction.* New York: HarperCollins, 2004.

On the Internet

Basics of Buddhism
http://www.pbs.org/edens/thailand/buddhism.htm

BBC Religions: Wesak
http://www.bbc.co.uk/religion/religions/buddhism/holydays/wesak.shtml

BBC Schools: Nirvana Day
http://www.bbc.co.uk/schools/religion/buddhism/nirvana.shtml

Buddhist Beliefs about the Afterlife
http://www.religionfacts.com/buddhism/beliefs/afterlife.htm#1

Buddhist Scriptures and Texts
http://www.religionfacts.com/buddhism/texts.htm

The Eightfold Path of Buddhism
http://www.dummies.com/how-to/content/the-eightfold-path-of-buddhism.html

His Holiness the 14th Dalai Lama of Tibet
http://www.dalailama.com

Metta Sutta
http://www.ling.upenn.edu/~beatrice/buddhist-practice/metta-sutta.html

Śanti Mantra
http://www.visiblemantra.org/shanti.html

Top 10 Celebrity Buddhists
http://www.wildmind.org/blogs/on-practice/top-10-celebrity-buddhists

A View on Buddhism: General Buddhist Symbols
http://viewonbuddhism.org/general_symbols_buddhism.html

abstain (ub-STAYN)—To give up a thing or activity

enlighten (en-LY-ten)—To instruct or shed light upon.

fast—To choose to go without food.

incense (IN-sense)—Perfume or smoke arising from a substance when it is burned.

mantra (MON-truh)—a word or phrase that is repeated over and over to help a person relax and meditate.

meditate (MEH-dih-tayt)—To engage in thought or reflection, often as part of religion.

Nirvana (nurr-VAH-nuh)—Freedom from the endless cycle of personal reincarnation; freedom from pain or worry.

precept (PREE-sept)—A commandment or direction to improve moral conduct.

reincarnation (ree-in-kar-NAY-shun)—The belief that when a person dies, he or she returns to Earth in another form hundreds to thousands of times.

shrine (SHRYNE)—A place devoted to a holy person, deity, or saint.

Tibetan Buddhist monks doing a sand painting

Bodhisatta   24–26

Buddha   8, 12–14

Buddhism

   church   8

   Dharma wheel   22

   diet   6–7

   enlightenment   14, 31

   Four Noble Truths   14

   incense   32

   karma   30

   mantra   33–34

   meditation   18, 32–33

   Noble Eightfold Path   8, 16, 20–22, 33

   promises   14–15

   reincarnation   29–31

   shrines   28, 29, 30–32

   spread of   14

   Tripitaka   23

Emerson, Ralph Waldo   17

Haeinsa Temple   23

Jataka Tales   23–24

King Ashoka   17

Lama, Dalai   35

Maitripa College   38

Metta Sutta   9

Nirvana Day   27

Siddhartha Gautama   12–14 (and see Buddha)

Three Treasures   32

Vesak Day   27

Well, H.G.   17

Whitman, Waldo   17

Tamra Orr is a full-time author living in the Pacific Northwest. She has a degree in English and Education from Ball State University and has written over 350 nonfiction books for all readers. She loves to read, write, and go camping. Orr moved to Oregon in 2001 for many reasons, including the amazing religious diversity of the region.